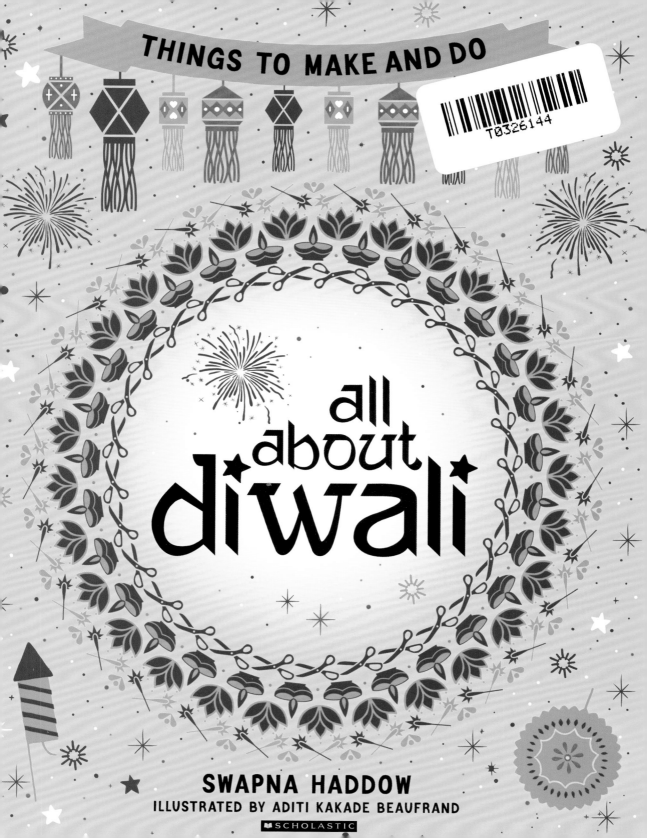

THINGS TO MAKE AND DO

T0326144

all about diwali

SWAPNA HADDOW
ILLUSTRATED BY ADITI KAKADE BEAUFRAND

SCHOLASTIC

FOR ME BECAUSE NOBODY LOVES DIWALI BURFI MORE THAN ME — SH

I DEDICATE THIS BOOK TO MY INDIAN HERITAGE,
FAMILY AND FRIENDS. SHUBH DEEPAVALI! — AKB

Published in the UK by Scholastic, 2021

1 London Bridge, London, SE1 9BG
Scholastic Ireland, 89E Lagan Road, Dublin Industrial Estate,
Glasnevin, Dublin, D11 HP5F

SCHOLASTIC and associated logos are trademarks and/or registered
trademarks of Scholastic Inc.

Text © Swapna Haddow, 2021
Illustrations by Aditi Kakade Beaufrand, © Scholastic, 2021

ISBN 978 0702 30959 5

A CIP catalogue record for this book is available from the British Library.

Printed in China

Paper made from wood grown in sustainable forests
and other controlled sources.

3 5 7 9 10 8 6 4 2

www.scholastic.co.uk

This copy of

all about diwali: things to make and do

belongs to:

_____

_____

Learn all about the Diwali festivals celebrated by millions
of Hindus, Sikhs, Jains and Buddhists all over the world
every year, and the events that lead up to them!

This book is packed full of crafts and delicious recipes
for you to make and share with friends and family.

Don't forget: you can find definitions of the words
in **bold** in the glossary at the back of the book.

diwali around
the world

Diwali is a festival celebrated by billions of people around the world, although it first originated in India. It is celebrated by many Hindus, Sikhs, Jains and Buddhists.

As you can imagine there are lots of different Diwali stories and countless ways that Diwali is observed, though good overcoming evil and light finding its way through darkness is central to all celebrations.

The festival is also known as Deepavali, which is the Sanskrit word for "row of lights". The city of Ayodhya in India once earned a Guinness World Record for lighting 300,000 lamps for Diwali.

Each year, the date of Diwali changes but the festival usually happens sometime in October or November.

DID YOU KNOW?

There are approximately 1.2 billion Hindus living around the world, with over a million Hindus living in the UK.

There are around 30 million Sikhs worldwide and over 80% live in India.

Almost 10% of the world's population practise Buddhism.

all about diwali

hindu diwali

Hinduism is one of the oldest religions in the world. It is based on an ancient, sacred text called the **Vedas**. Hinduism is a religion of many gods but Hindus believe that there is one supreme being of which the gods are incarnations.

With over a billion Hindus worldwide, people come together to observe Diwali for many different reasons, but the idea of good vanquishing evil and light finding its way through darkness is a common theme. Here are some of the more popular Hindu stories behind Diwali:

the legend of
rama and sita

Long ago, in the Indian city of Ayodhya, Prince Rama was getting ready to take the throne, as his father had become ill.

However, his stepmother had other ideas and before Rama could be crowned king, she commanded that he be banished from the kingdom for fourteen years so her son could be king instead. Rama, his wife Sita and his brother Lakshman obediently left Ayodhya, much to the dismay of the people of Ayodhya who adored the prince.

Rama, Sita and Lakshman lived happily for many years in the forest. But when the two demons King Ravana and his sister Shurpanakha arrived, their troubles began.

The ten-headed Ravana kidnapped Sita and trapped her in his palace on the island of Lanka.

Rama and Lakshman set out to rescue her immediately. They were aided on their journey by the monkey king, Hanuman, whose army of monkeys helped the brothers build a bridge to the island of Lanka and find Sita.

A huge deadly battle broke out as Rama took on Ravana, but with good on his side he defeated the evil king and rescued Sita.

By this time, Rama's banishment was over and it was time to return to Ayodhya to take his place as the rightful king. The people of the kingdom were overjoyed to have their prince return and lit his way home with candles and clay **diyas**, which is why the lighting of diyas is so important at Diwali.

the legend of
krishna

The gods were in despair as the world was in turmoil. Narakasura, who had been granted immortality by the gods, spent his days terrorising the people of the Earth.

The gods pleaded with Krishna and his wife, Satyabhama, to face the demon in a huge battle.

Krishna fought hard and weakened Narakasura, but could not vanquish him because of his immortality. But when Satyabhama saw Krishna hurt on the battlefield, she shot a fatal arrow, which took Narakasura down.

Her shot succeeded because when Narakasura had been granted immortality he had asked that he would never meet his end at the hands of men. However, as Satyabhama was a woman she was able to kill the power-hungry Narakasura.

After the battle, Krishna and Satyabhama were bathed in scented oils to remove the scars of the battle and so, in remembrance of this, oil lamps are lit at Diwali.

hindu diwali
celebrations

Hindus celebrate Diwali in many different ways. Practices vary from family to family and Diwali is often celebrated over a number of days. Each day holds its own significance and its own celebration, but over the entire festive period, tiny clay lamps called **diyas** are lit and firework displays are common.

dhanteras:

Dhanteras marks the day the Goddess Lakshmi is worshipped. Hindus pray to her for good luck and wealth. They prepare their homes for Lakshmi by cleaning and decorating with diyas and colourful powdered patterns called **rangoli**. Prayers include a Lakshmi **puja** where light, flowers and sweets are offered to the goddess.

Diwali is considered a good time to make big purchases so it's not unusual to see queues at the local car showroom or shopping centre on Dhanteras. Families exchange gifts and money and share stories of Diwali celebrations gone by.

naraka chaturdashi:

On Naraka Chaturdashi, Hindus remember the legend of Krishna (see page 8). They add aromatic oils to their baths and wear new clothes. Firecrackers are often lit, and children are given sparklers to wave.

sikh diwali

Sikhism was founded by a holy teacher called Guru Nanak around 1500. Sikhs believe in one God and in everybody being equal. They follow the teachings and hymns of their holy book **Guru Granth Sahib**.

Bandi Chhor Divas, celebrated on Diwali, commemorates the release of the sixth Sikh guru, Guru Hargobind from prison in 1619.

Emperor Jahangir, who had imprisoned Guru Hargobind, agreed to his release but Guru Hargobind only agreed to leave if the fifty-two warriors who had been imprisoned with him were released too. The emperor said yes but only for those who could hold onto the guru's cloak tail as he left the prison.

Guru Hargobind cleverly made a cloak with fifty-two pieces of string and so each warrior was able to hold on to one string and leave the prison alongside him.

SIKH DIWALI CLEBRATIONS

Sikhs will often attend the **gurdwara** to remember Guru Hargobind through prayer. They will light candles to illuminate their homes and join in a shared meal, or **langar**, made in the communal kitchen of the gurdwara, which is also called the langar.

jain diwali

Unlike some religions, Jains do not believe in a god. Jainism, which was made popular by the teachings of Mahavira in the sixth century BCE, is based on the idea that people should never be violent in what they think or do.

In Jainism, Diwali celebrates Mahavira's attainment of moksha, which means his soul was finally free from the human cycle of birth and death.

Jains light lamps and share sweets on Diwali to remember Mahavira. And many celebrate by singing hymns and giving to charity. As the day after Diwali marks the Jain New Year, this is a chance to get together and celebrate new beginnings.

buddhist diwali

Buddhism is founded on the teachings of Siddhartha Gautama, who was called the Buddha.

Buddhists do not believe in God but rather the idea of enlightenment and finding peace through prayer and meditation.

For Buddhists, Diwali marks the day Emperor Ashoka converted to Buddhism. On this day, **monasteries** and Buddhist temples are decorated, and Buddhists will go to the temple to spend time in prayer and contemplation.

diwali gifts

Giving to charity is one thing all Diwali celebrations have in common. Peace and kindness are an essential part of all Diwali festivities and donating money and time are important too.

At the international border between India and Pakistan, soldiers from the two countries give each other traditional sweets as a gesture of peace and kindness.

Children often receive presents of money and new clothes, with traditional **kurtas** and **dhotis** for boys and **lehenga cholis** and **salwar kameez** for girls. Grown-up men might wear a **sherwani** coat with their kurta and women will often wear a **sari** and bangles they've received as gifts.

art and crafts

make a diwali card

It is traditional to celebrate Diwali by sending good wishes to family, friends and neighbours. These cards are a brilliant way to send your special Diwali messages.

you will need:

- A4 coloured card
- A pen or pencil
- Glitter
- Glue
- Colouring pens and pencils
- Scissors

SAFETY FIRST

Ask an adult for help when using scissors.

instructions:

1. First, take your A4 coloured card and fold it in half.

2. Draw the shape of a lit diya, making sure one side of the diya sits on the fold (as shown here).

3. Cut carefully along the outside line, but take care not to cut along the fold.

4. Open up your card. It looks like a diya!

5. Decorate the front of your card by colouring in the diya with bright colours and using glitter to decorate the flame.

6. Now you can write a Diwali message inside and give your card to someone special.

HAPPY DIWALI

LOTS OF LOVE

TOP TIP:

You can make smaller diyas and use these as decorative placeholders at your Diwali feast. Just add the name of your guest on the outside of their card.

diwali fan decorations

Every household celebrating Diwali decorates their home to welcome good fortune. Here are some fun decoration ideas to add colour and Diwali cheer to your home.

you will need:

- Two equal size squares of coloured or patterned paper – origami or wrapping paper works well
- Stapler
- Sticky tape
- Coloured ribbon

instructions:

1. Fold over 2 cm of paper, making a sharp crease along the fold.

2. Flip the paper over and make another 2 cm fold.

3. Keeping flipping over and folding, creating a concertina of folded paper.

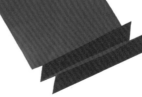

4. Now fold the strip in half and staple the two inside edges together. You will see you have made a semi-circle concertina.

5. Repeat steps 1–3 with the second square of paper.

6. Stick the two edges of the semi-circles together using sticky tape – you will find you have a circular fan shape.

7. Attach a length of ribbon to the tip of one folded fan. You can now hang your Diwali fan decoration.

TOP TIP:

Make fans in different sizes and hang them from different lengths of ribbons for an impressive display.

diwali bunting

This colourful bunting uses a similar technique to the concertina fans and looks just as festive strung up around your house.

you will need:

- A4 yellow and orange card or paper
- Glue stick
- Sticky tape
- Coloured ribbon

instructions:

1. Fold over 2 cm of card, making a sharp crease along the fold.

2. Flip the card over and make another 2 cm fold.

3. Keep flipping over and folding, creating a concertina of folded card.

4. Now fold the strip in half.

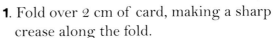

5. Glue the two ends together and you will see the shape of a semi-circle diya take form.

6. Cut a teardrop shape from yellow card and a smaller teardrop shape from orange card.

7. Glue the smaller teardrop on top of the larger teardrop to make a flame. Attach the flame to the centre of the diya with sticky tape.

8. Repeat steps 1–7 until you have as many diyas as you want.

9. Using the sticky tape, attach the diyas at equal intervals along the length of the ribbon.

10. String the bunting up in your house.

diwali lantern

Light is such an important part of Diwali celebrations and this lantern will really brighten up your home.

you will need:

- Clean glass jar
- Scissors
- PVA glue
- A tablespoon
- Food colouring
- Black paper or card
- Paintbrushes
- A battery-powered tea light candle

SAFETY FIRST

Ask an adult for help when using scissors.

instructions:

1. Make sure your glass jar is completely clean and dry.

2. Pour approximately one tablespoon of glue on to a plate and mix in a few  drops of food colouring. Then repeat this step for as many colours as you like.

3. Using a paintbrush, add the colours to the jar by creating bands of colours that blend into one another.

4. Cut out teardrop shapes (as shown here) using the scissors and black paper. Cut the outer shape first and then carefully cut out a smaller shape inside. You could use a hole punch to create patterns in each one, too.

5. Stick the shapes to the outside of the jar.

6. Once the glue has dried, you can place a tea light inside and watch the multi-coloured light shine.

make a diya

you will need:

- Air-drying clay (you can find this in craft shops or ask an adult to buy it for you online)
- Rolling pin
- Large round cookie cutter
- Small bowl
- Poster paints
- A battery-powered tea light candle

instructions:

1. Roll out the air-drying clay.

2. Using a large cookie cutter, cut out a circle in the clay.

3. Place the clay circle into the small bowl to form the shape of the diya.

4. Allow the clay to dry overnight. You can use this time to think about fun designs for your diya.

5. Remove the clay diya from the bowl and let it dry completely.

6. Once dry, paint the diya in bright colours.

7. Add the candle to the diya and let light shine at your Diwali celebrations.

TOP TIP:

Before placing the clay diya in the small bowl you can use a stamp to create patterns in the clay. You can even use beads and gems to decorate the clay before letting your diya set overnight.

make a diwali rocket

Diwali conjures up images of bright, colourful firework displays that light up the night sky and crackers that smoke and snap in the streets. However, if you can't get to your local firework display or you are looking for a less noisy way to celebrate, especially if you have pets at home, here is a quiet and eco-friendly alternative to fireworks.

you will need:

- Coloured tissue paper
- PVA glue
- Paintbrush
- Small cardboard tube – the inside of a tissue roll works well
- Coloured card
- Stapler
- Lolly stick or wooden skewers
- Glitter
- Star stickers

instructions:

1. Using the glue and paintbrush, wrap and glue a layer of coloured tissue paper around the cardboard tube.

2. Cut out a 10 cm diameter circle from the card and then cut the circle in half to make two semi-circles.

3. Curl one of the semi-circles into a cone shape by overlapping the edges. Staple along edge to hold the shape of the cone.

4. Glue the cone on to one end of the tube. You've made your rocket shape! Glue the wooden stick to the other end of the tube and leave your rocket to dry.

5. Once it has dried, it's time to decorate your rocket. Use the star stickers and glitter to make your rocket sparkle like a firework.

6. Cut strips of tissue paper and attach to the open end of the rocket tube to create flames.

7. Your colourful rockets are finished and ready to be part of your Diwali decorations.

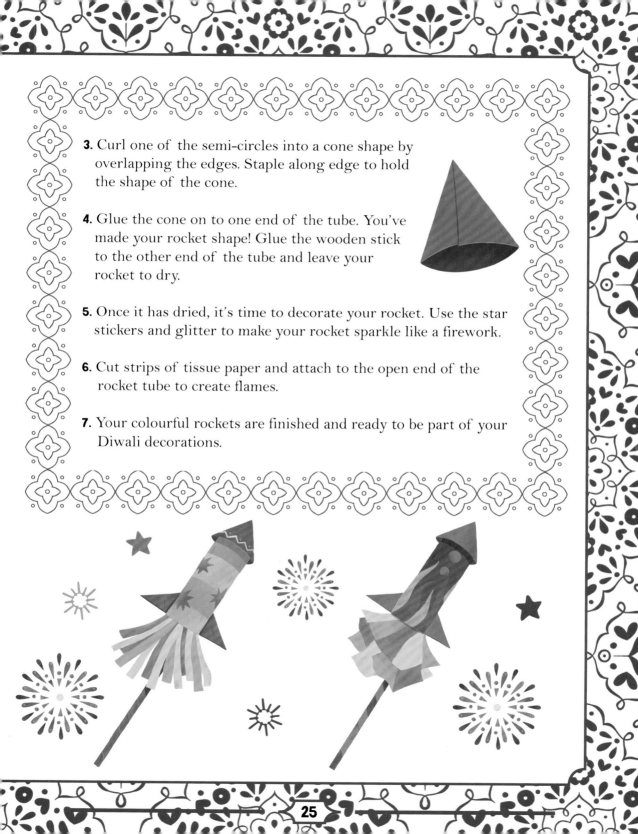

rangoli

Decorate the outside of your home with coloured sand and chalk, also known as rangoli. This is a common art form in India where you will often see elaborate designs of flowers and geometric patterns outside temples and homes.

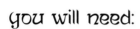

you will need:

- Sand
- Coloured powder paint
- A tablespoon
- Sealable bags
- Chalk

instructions:

1. Spoon eight heaped tablespoons of slightly damp sand into a sealable bag.

2. Add two tablespoons of powder paint into the bag.

3. Seal the bag tight and shake hard until all the powder paint and sand mix together.

4. Open the bag carefully and let the coloured sand dry out.

5. Repeat steps 1–4 with as many colours as you like.

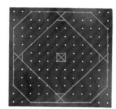

6. While the coloured sand dries, draw a grid of dots on the ground just outside your home with chalk. The grid should be about 40 cm by 40 cm with 4 cm gaps between dots.

7. Now join up the dots to create a design. Try to keep this symmetrical to create a simple rangoli design.

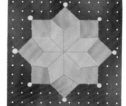

8. Once the coloured sand is dry, reseal the bag and carefully make a tiny cut in the corner of the bag. Try not to let the powder stream out of the bag before you are ready to fill in your design!

9. Carefully let the powder pour out of the cut to fill in your rangoli design, using the different colours you created to complete your design.

diwali table centrepiece

Family, friends and neighbours will often feast together to celebrate Diwali. This fun table centrepiece idea will be the talk of your Diwali meal.

you will need:

- Five disposable cups
- Small container
- Coloured tissue paper
- PVA glue
- Water
- Glitter
- Colouring pens

instructions:

1. Tear the tissue paper into small squares.

2. Mix equal amounts of glue and water in a container to make a wet paste.

3. Dip the tissue paper squares in the paste and stick them to a cup, covering the outside and inside.

4. Let the cup dry.

5. Cut a few more squares and glue them to the inside to create a flame effect and let the cup dry again.

6. Once the glue is fully dry, decorate the cup with glitter and colouring pens if you wish.

7. Repeat steps 2–5 to create five cups to represent the five days of Diwali and group the cups together in the middle of a table to create a stunning festive centrepiece.

TOP TIP:

You can make as many cups as you want and then group them together to create a beautiful centrepiece.

diwali tableware

Here is an easy way to create festive Diwali cups. You can use this technique to add sparkle to plates, bowls and serving platters too.

you will need:

- Paper cups (coloured ones are ideal)
- Sticky gems
- Glitter washi tape
- Scissors

SAFETY FIRST

Ask an adult for help when using scissors.

instructions:

1. Cut your washi tape into different shapes such as diamonds, narrow strips and triangles. Stick the pieces of glitter washi tape to the outside of a cup. You can create patterns of zigzags or stripes.

2. Now stick colourful gems along the tape.

3. Create enough cups for all your guests to enjoy.

diwali sweet giftboxes

Mithai is the Hindi and Urdu word for sweets and no Diwali celebration is complete without a feast of colourful mithai. This easy-to-make egg carton mithai hamper will delight your Diwali guests.

you will need:

- Clean, empty egg cartons
- Paint
- Paintbrushes
- Glitter
- Baking paper
- Sweets
- Ribbon

instructions:

1. Make sure your egg carton is cleaned inside and out.

2. Paint the outside of the egg carton with bright colours and leave to dry. You can use glitter too.

3. Once dry, paint the inside of the egg carton with bright colours and leave to dry completely.

4. Cut small squares of baking paper and line each cell.

5. Fill each cell with sweets. You can fill the cartons with traditional mithai or your favourite party sweets – jelly beans and sugar-coated chocolate buttons are great for this.

6. Close the carton and tie with a ribbon. This is a wonderful gift that your guests will treasure.

recipes

SAFETY FIRST

Remember to ask an adult for help when using any sharp
equipment, such as knives, or attempting a recipe that
requires the use of an oven, hob or electric blender.
And have fun creating and sharing these delicious treats!

vegetable diyas

These simple, healthy edible diyas make a stunning display at any Diwali feast.

ingredients

- Cucumber
- Carrot

equipment

- A sharp knife

SAFETY FIRST

Ask an adult for help when using a knife.

method

1. Cut thin slices of cucumber and then cut the round slices in half to create the diya shape.

2. Cut thin slices of carrots and trim to create a flame shape.

3. Place the cucumber diyas on a plate and top with the carrot flames.

TOP TIP:

You can also make edible diyas from halved dried apples or cashew nuts and top them with almonds for flames.

potato curry

Yummy potato curry always goes down a treat at any Diwali feast.

serves: 4

ingredients

- 5 medium-sized potatoes
- 2 tomatoes
- Fresh ginger
- 1 onion
- 1 tsp cumin
- 1 tsp turmeric
- 2 tsp coriander powder
- 1 tsp garam masala
- 1 tbsp oil
- 1 tbsp fresh coriander
- 375 ml water
- 1 green chilli, chopped (optional)

equipment

- Vegetable peeler
- Sharp knife
- Chopping board
- Grater
- Saucepan
- Large spoon
- Fork
- Saucepan with lid

SAFETY FIRST
Ask an adult for help when using a knife or the hob/oven/cooker.

method

1. Peel and cut the potatoes into equal-sized chunks and set aside.

2. Cut the tomatoes into small pieces and set aside.

3. Chop the onion and set aside.

4. Grate the ginger until you have about a tablespoon.

5. Heat the oil in a saucepan and add the onions, chopped chilli (optional) and ginger. Cook until the onions are soft.

6. Now add the spices. Stir and cook for another minute, then add the tomatoes and mix through.

7. Add the potatoes and water and bring to the boil.

8. Leave to simmer for 20 minutes or until the potatoes are tender. You can check if the potatoes are tender by seeing if they are easily pierced with a fork.

9. Garnish with chopped fresh coriander.

chappatis

A chappati, also known as roti, is a flatbread commonly eaten with meals in India.

ingredients

- 200 g wholemeal flour
- 150 ml lukewarm water
- 1 tbsp oil
- 1 tbsp softened butter

equipment

- Rolling pin
- Non-stick frying pan
- Large bowl
- Tea towel

SAFETY FIRST
Ask an adult for help when using the hob/oven or the cooker.

method

1. Add the flour to a large bowl and make a well in the centre.

2. Add the oil and gradually pour in the water, mixing the ingredients together with your hands.

3. Cover the bowl with a tea towel or lid and leave for 15 minutes.

4. Spread some oil on your hands and knead the dough once more for a minute.

5. Tear off a ping-pong ball-sized piece of dough and roll flat with a rolling pin. You should create a circle around 15 cm wide.

6. Heat the frying pan.

7. Carefully drop the first chappati onto the dry pan and heat it until you see bubbles form on the surface. That's when you need to flip the chappati over and cook the other side. Chappatis don't need more than a minute or so to cook on each side.

8. Brush the cooked chappati with a little bit of butter and it is ready to serve.

TOP TIP:

Keep the chappatis warm by covering them with a clean tea towel until you are ready to eat.

spiced rice with peas

serves: 4

ingredients

- 200 g basmati rice
- 2 tbsp oil
- 1 white onion
- 2 cloves
- 3 green cardamom pods
- 1 cinnamon stick
- ½ tsp cumin
- ¼ tsp turmeric
- 50 g frozen peas
- 550 ml water

SAFETY FIRST

Ask an adult for help when using a knife, or the hob/oven/cooker.

equipment

- Sieve
- Saucepan and lid
- Microwave-safe bowl
- Chopping board
- Sharp knife
- Large spoon

method

1. Wash the rice using a sieve over a bowl of water, swishing it with your hands to help clear. Strain and put aside.

2. Chop the onion and cook in the oil in the saucepan until soft and brown.

3. Add the cloves, cardamom, cinnamon stick, cumin and turmeric and stir, cooking for another minute.

4. Add the washed rice and water and put the lid on the pan, leaving the rice to come to the boil. This should take about 10 minutes.

5. In the meantime, put the peas in a microwave-safe bowl and heat in a microwave for 2 to 3 minutes until hot. Be very careful when removing the bowl from the microwave and ask an adult to help you if it is too hot.

6. The rice should have soaked up all the water and be soft and fluffy when cooked. Spoon into a bowl and mix in the peas, ready to serve to your guests.

TOP TIP:

You can add in chopped fried peppers in addition to the peas or as an alternative to peas.

milk peda

These popular milk fudge sweets are so easy to make and delicious to eat. They are a must-have for any Diwali banquet.

ingredients

- 110 g butter
- 395 g sweetened condensed milk
- 170 g milk powder
- ¼ tsp cardamom powder
- Chopped pistachio nuts or edible silver paper for decoration (optional)

SAFETY FIRST

Ask an adult for help when using a knife.

equipment

- Microwave-proof bowl
- Floral cookie stamp (optional)
- Table knife
- Large spoon

method

1. Cut the butter into chunks and let it sit at room temperature in a microwave-proof bowl until the butter becomes soft. This can take up to 60 minutes.

2. Once the butter is soft, mix in the condensed milk.

3. Put the mixture in the microwave for 2 minutes. The mixture will start to bubble.

4. Mix in the milk powder and cook in the microwave for a further minute.

5. Stir in the cardamon powder and cook in the microwave for another minute.

6. The mixture should come together like a dough. When it is cool enough to touch, make small walnut size balls with the dough.

7. You can use a floral or patterned cookie stamp to create a pattern on the dough balls by pressing into the dough with the stamp.

8. Place the milk pedas on a plate to share with your family and friends.

TOP TIP:

Decorate the top of the milk peda with chopped pistachio nuts or edible silver paper.

chocolate burfi

ingredients

- 500 g milk powder
- 470 ml double cream
- 200 g sugar
- 80 g dark chocolate chips
- 2 tsp unsweetened cocoa powder

equipment

- Microwave-safe bowl
- Baking tray
- Baking paper
- Whisk
- Table knife

method

1. Add the milk powder, cream and sugar into the microwave-safe bowl and whisk until fully blended.

2. Place the bowl in the microwave and heat for 2 minutes. Be careful when removing the bowl from the microwave as it may be very hot.

3. Whisk the mixture well to get rid of any lumps.

4. Repeat steps 2 and 3 four more times until the mixture has been cooked for 8 minutes. The mixture should come together to make a dough.

5. Once the dough has cooled, knead it for a couple of minutes until soft.

6. Line the baking tray with baking paper.

7. Spread half of the dough over the baking paper.

8. Add cocoa powder and chocolate chips to the remaining half of the dough and microwave it for 30 seconds.

9. Once the chocolate dough has cooled, knead it until it is soft.

10. Lay the chocolate dough on top of the white dough and spread it evenly so it covers the white dough completely.

11. Allow the burfi mixture to cool before putting it in the fridge for about three hours so it can set. Once completely cooled and set, cut the burfi into squares and serve at room temperature.

coconut burfi

ingredients

- 250 ml sweetened condensed milk
- 250 g icing sugar
- 200 g desiccated coconut
- Pink food colouring

equipment

- Baking tray
- Bowl
- Spoon
- Table knife

SAFETY FIRST
Ask an adult for help when using a knife.

method

1. Mix the condensed milk and sugar in a bowl.

2. Add in the coconut and bring the mixture together to form a dough.

3. Put half the dough in another bowl.

4. Add a couple drops of pink food colouring to one half of the mixture and mix in well. Take care not to get any food colouring on your hands as it can stain them.

5. Spread the pink mixture out into the baking tray.

6. Spread the white burfi mixture over the pink, covering it completely.

7. Leave to set overnight in the fridge.

8. Once set, cut the burfi into squares, ready to eat!

almond halwa

ingredients

- 75 g blanched and peeled almonds
- 470 ml water
- 5 green cardamom pods
- 4 strands of saffron
- 120 ml milk
- 55 g coconut oil
- 100 g caster sugar

equipment

- Electric blender
- Saucepan
- Mortar and pestle
- Spoon

SAFETY FIRST
Ask an adult for help when using an electric blender, or oven/hob/cooker.

method

1. Blend the almonds with the water to make a smooth paste in the electric blender.

2. Pour the paste into a saucepan and stir carefully until it thickens and leaves the sides. This can take ten minutes. Ask an adult to help you with the hob.

3. Crush the cardamom pods with a mortar and pestle.

4. Add the crushed cardamom pods, sugar, milk, oil and saffron to the almond paste and stir well until the ingredients combine into a soft dough.

5. You can spoon out the halwa into bowls or roll into small, walnut-sized balls once cooled.

cashew katli

Unlike burfi and halwa, katli does not use milk but it's just as delicious and fudge-like as burfi.

ingredients

- 150 g cashew nuts
- 100 g sugar
- 5 tbsp water
- 1 tbsp butter
- 4 strands saffron

equipment

- Electric blender or coffee grinder
- Saucepan
- Greased baking tray
- Table knife

SAFETY FIRST
Ask an adult for help when using a knife or an electric blender or coffee grinder or the hob/oven/cooker.

method

1. Blend the cashew nuts in an electric blender or a coffee grinder. When you are finished you should have a powder.

2. Heat the sugar and water in a saucepan. Once the sugar is fully dissolved, mix in the cashew nut powder.

3. Cook the mixture for 10 minutes until it thickens.

4. Add the butter and the saffron to the mixture, stirring continuously.

5. Once the mixture comes together as a dough, take off the heat and spread in the greased baking tray.

6. Allow the dough to cool before cutting into squares or diamonds.

7. Cool in the fridge for a further two hours before serving.

TOP TIP:
Decorate the top of the sweets with edible silver paper.

bliss ball laddoos

These easy-to-make, healthy option laddoos make a delicious snack, even when it's not Diwali.

ingredients

- 220 g pitted dates
- 30 g sunflower seeds
- 3 tbsp chia seeds
- 1 tsp vanilla extract
- 2 tbsp cocoa powder
- 2 tbsp coconut oil
- 40 g desiccated coconut

equipment

- Large bowl

method

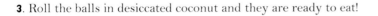

1. Mix the dates, seeds, vanilla extract, cocoa powder and oil together in a bowl with your hands until the mixture comes together.

2. Roll into walnut-sized balls.

3. Roll the balls in desiccated coconut and they are ready to eat!

diwali biscuits

ingredients

- 230 g plain flour
- ½ tsp bicarbonate of soda
- ¼ tsp salt
- 115 g butter
- 100 g caster sugar
- 1 egg
- 1 tsp vanilla extract

for the icing

- 1 egg white
- 1 tsp lemon juice
- 200 g icing sugar
- Food colouring (for decoration)

equipment

- Baking tray
- Baking paper
- Cookie cutters
- Cooling rack
- Two large bowls
- Several small bowls
- Large spoon
- Whisk
- Cling film
- Teaspoon

SAFETY FIRST
Ask an adult for help when using the oven/cooker.

method

1. Mix the flour, salt and bicarbonate of soda in a large bowl.

2. In a separate bowl, beat the butter and sugar together until the mixture is light and fluffy.

3. Add the egg and vanilla extract to the butter-sugar mixture and whisk.

4. Add the mixture to the flour and mix until it comes together in a dough.

5. Wrap the dough in cling film and leave in the fridge for 4 hours. In the meantime, pre-heat the oven to 180 °C.

6. Line a baking tray with baking paper.

7. Once the dough has chilled, remove from the cling film and roll the dough to about 1 cm in thickness.

8. Cut the dough using cookie cutters and place on the baking paper.

9. Bake for approximately 10 minutes, until the edges are lightly browned.

10. Carefully remove the tray from the oven using oven gloves and cool the biscuits on a cooling rack.

11. While the biscuits cool, you can make the icing. Whisk the egg white and lemon juice for a minute.

12. Sift the icing sugar into the mixture and whisk for a further 2–3 minutes.

13. Portion the icing mixture into separate bowls and add a drop of food colouring to each bowl to create an array of colours to paint the biscuits with.

14. Using a small spoon, decorate the cooled biscuits with the different colours of icing in rangoli patterns.

mini fruity firecrackers

These firecrackers are healthy and super-easy to make (and eat!).
They're pet-friendly too, unlike noisy real-life firecrackers.

ingredients

- Grapes
- Strawberries
- Blueberries

equipment

- Decorative cocktail sticks

method

1. Wash and dry the fruit.

2. Thread the grapes and blueberries on to the cocktail sticks leaving the tip free.

3. Add a strawberry to the top of each skewer to finish your rocket.

breadstick sparklers

These simple, edible sparklers are a brilliant alternative for younger siblings and friends who are not ready for real sparklers on Diwali night.

ingredients

- Breadsticks
- Chocolate
- Hundreds and thousands
- Water

equipment

- Saucepan
- Bowl

SAFETY FIRST
Ask an adult for help when using the hob/oven/cooker.

method

1. Melt the chocolate in a bowl over a saucepan of hot water.

2. Dip the breadsticks in the melted chocolate.

3. Sprinkle hundreds and thousands over the chocolate to finish each sparkler and leave to set.

pistachio kulfi

Similar to ice cream, kulfi is a popular dessert in India. These cool, refreshing milky ice lollies are perfect after a feast of spicy Diwali treats.

ingredients

- 3 litres milk
- 100 g sugar

for the pistachio paste

- 35 g cashew nuts
- 40 g blanched and peeled almonds
- 40 g shelled pistachios
- 2 tsp cardamom powder
- ½ tsp cinnamon powder
- 1 tbsp water

equipment

- Electric blender
- Large saucepan
- Large spoon
- Kulfi or lolly moulds
- Lolly sticks

SAFETY FIRST

Ask an adult for help when using an electric blender or the hob/ oven/cooker.

method

1. Blend the cashew nuts, almonds, pistachios, cardamom and cinnamon in a blender to create a paste. Add a little water if needed.

2. Pour the milk in the saucepan and heat, bringing it to the boil.

3. Once the milk boils, reduce the heat and simmer for 30 minutes. The milk should reduce by half.

4. Add sugar and mix with a large spoon.

5. Now add the pistachio paste and whisk well.

6. Take the mixture off the heat and let it cool completely.

7. Pour the mixture into the kulfi or lolly moulds and leave in the freezer for 15 hours. Remember to add the lolly sticks into the moulds when the mixture has partially set.

frozen chocolate bananas

ingredients

- 3 ripe bananas
- 170 g chocolate chips
- Chopped hazelnuts
- Water
- Desiccated coconuts
- Sprinkles

equipment

- Saucepan
- Lolly sticks or wooden skewers
- Baking tray

SAFETY FIRST
Ask an adult for help when using the hob/oven/cooker.

method

1. Peel the bananas and cut in half crosswise (rather than lengthwise). You should have six halves.

2. Insert a lolly stick or wooden skewer into the flat end of the banana and place each banana half on a baking tray.

3. Put the baking tray in the freezer and leave for 2 hours.

4. Once the bananas are frozen, melt the chocolate chips in a bowl over a pan of hot water. Be very careful as the bowl can slip around.

5. Dip the frozen bananas in the melted chocolate, using a spoon to make sure you cover the top of the banana fully with chocolate.

6. Quickly sprinkle the chocolate with chopped hazelnuts, sprinkles and desiccated coconut pieces. The chocolate will harden almost as soon as it touches the frozen banana.

7. Serve immediately or store in the freezer for serving later.

spiced chai milk

Chai is a spiced black tea popular in India all year round. This caffeine-free recipe is a warm and delicious alternative to tea.

ingredients

- A glass of milk
- 2 tsp sugar
- ¼ tsp ground cinnamon
- A pinch of ground nutmeg
- A pinch of ground cloves

SAFETY FIRST
Ask an adult for help when using the hob/oven/cooker.

equipment

- Small saucepan
- Whisk

method

1. Pour half of the milk into a saucepan.

2. Add the spices and sugar and whisk together, bringing the mixture to the boil.

3. Turn down the heat and add the rest of the milk, simmering for a minute.

4. Pour into your favourite mug and enjoy!

strawberry and rose slushie

ingredients

- 100 g raspberries
- 100 g strawberries
- 1 handful of crushed ice
- 400 ml unsweetened coconut milk
- 2 tbsp agave nectar
- 1 tsp rosewater
- 50 ml sparkling water (chilled)

method

1. Mix the raspberries and strawberries with crushed ice in a tall glass.

2. Mix the coconut milk, agave nectar and rosewater in a jug.

3. Pour the coconut milk mixture over the fruit and ice and top with sparkling water.

4. Stir and garnish with sliced strawberries.

lychee cooler

ingredients

- 10 peeled and pitted lychees
  (ask an adult to help peel and pit them for you)
- 200 ml coconut water
- A sprig of mint leaves
- 2 handfuls of ice cubes

equipment

- Electric blender

SAFETY FIRST

Ask an adult for help when using an electric blender.

method

1. Crush the ice cubes in a blender for 20 seconds.

2. Add the lychees and coconut water into the blender and blend for a further 20 seconds.

3. Pour into a glass and garnish with mint leaves and lychees.

diwali rainbow milkshake

ingredients

- Milk
- Vanilla ice cream
- Pink food colouring
- Blue food colouring
- Purple food colouring
- Whipped cream
- Hundreds and thousands
- Marshmallows
- Sweets

equipment

- Electric blender
- Large serving glass

SAFETY FIRST
Ask an adult for help when using an electric blender.

method

1. Add one part milk to three parts ice cream in a blender.

2. Add a couple of drops of pink food colouring into the blender and blend until smooth.

3. Pour the pink milkshake into a large glass.

4. Repeat steps 1–3 with the purple food colouring and then the blue food colouring.

5. Top the rainbow milkshake with whipped cream, marshmallows, hundreds and thousands and sweets.

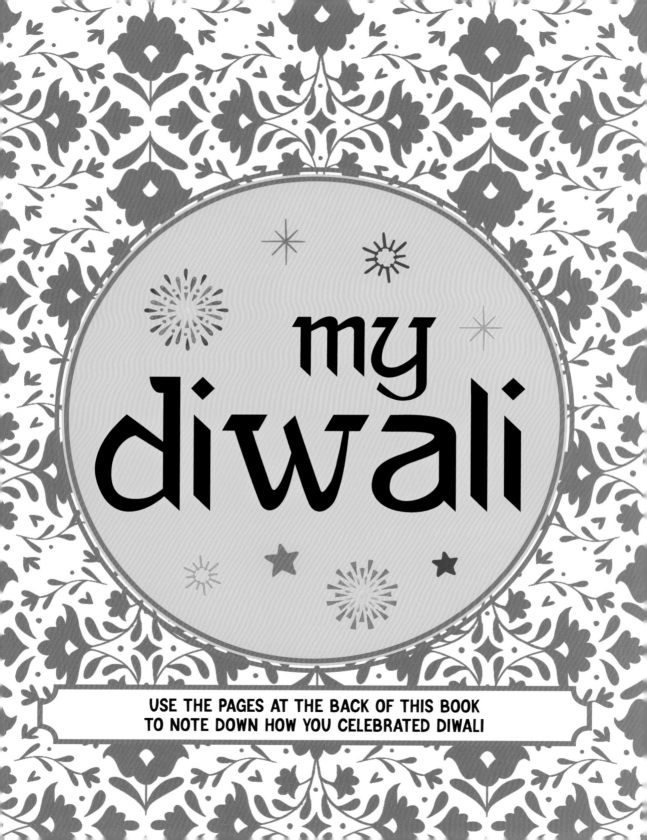

my diwali

USE THE PAGES AT THE BACK OF THIS BOOK
TO NOTE DOWN HOW YOU CELEBRATED DIWALI

my diwali journal

Use this space to keep a record of any special Diwali memories.

date _____

i spent diwali with _____

my favourite part of the day was:

_____

_____

_____

_____

_____

draw a picture of your diwali celebration below!

my goals for
the coming year

You can use this page to write down three things you would like to do in the next year.

Perhaps you are going to help out around the house more or perhaps you are going to pick up litter in the park or at the beach. Perhaps you might try and learn a new skill or sport.

Whatever you choose, remember to check on the list over the coming year to make sure you are keeping up with your goals.

notes

glossary

BANDI CHHOR DIVAS: roughly translates to "prisoner release day" and is the name given to the Sikh Diwali celebration.

DHOTI: a long piece of material tied over the waist to cover the legs.

DIYA: a clay candle holder.

GURDWARA: the Sikh place of worship.

GURU: a spiritual teacher.

GURU GRANTH SAHIB: the Sikh holy book.

KURTA: a loose collarless shirt worn over drawstring pyjama bottoms.

LEHENGHA CHOLI: a matching top with long skirt and shawl.

LANGAR: the community kitchen of a gurdwara where free meals are made and shared.

MITHAI: sweets often made with butter, ghee, milk and sugar.

MONASTERY (BUDDHIST): a building where people live and devote their time and life to their faith.

RANGOLI: colourful patterns made from powder and chalk.

PUJA: prayer ritual.

SALWAR KAMEEZ: drawstring pyjama bottoms worn under a long tunic or dress.

SARI: a long length of material draped over the body and worn by women.

SHERWANI: a long coat worn with a kurta or kurta bottoms.

REINCARNATION: this is a key belief in Hinduism, Jainism, Sikhism and Buddhism. These religions teach that all living things go through a cycle of birth, life, death and rebirth. This continuous cycle of rebirth is known as reincarnation.

VEDAS: the Hindu holy scriptures.

about the author

SWAPNA HADDOW is a children's writer who lives in New Zealand with her husband, her son and their dog, Archie. She loves reading, crafts and eating mithai which is why the book is packed with all three.

about the illustrator

ADITI KAKADE BEAUFRAND is an Indian illustrator based in France. She likes experimenting with bright, happy colours. She grew up reading fairytales, watching animated films, imagining adventure stories and likewise her style is an embodiment of her Indian heritage and western culture. She loves animals and taking long walks on the beach but is never too far away from a pencil and a paper to draw her perception of the world.

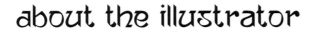